Original Six Era: The Rise of the Chicago Blackhawks Dynasty

Lloyd Green

Published by Lloyd Green, 2023.

ORIGINAL SIX ERA: THE RISE OF THE CHICAGO BLACKHAWKS DYNASTY

First edition. October 31, 2023.

ISBN: 979-8223103967

Written by Lloyd Green.

Also by Lloyd Green

Original Six Era: The Rise of the Chicago Blackhawks Dynasty

Table of Contents

Original Six Era: The Rise of the Chicago Blackhawks Dynasty

Origins and Early Years: The Birth of the Blackhawks and Their Foundational Era

In the bustling city of Chicago, 1926 marked the dawn of a new era, one intertwined with passion, ice, and the roar of the crowd. That year, the Chicago Blackhawks soared into existence, not merely as a hockey team but as an embodiment of the Windy City's spirit.

The birth of the Blackhawks was, in many ways, a testament to Chicago's burgeoning love affair with sports. Major Frederic McLaughlin, a former commander in World War I and heir to a coffee fortune, was instrumental in establishing the franchise. Upon acquiring the Portland Rosebuds, a defunct team from the Western Hockey League, McLaughlin brought them to Chicago, renaming them the "Black Hawks" in tribute to the Black Hawk Division he served in during the war. (It wasn't until 1986 that the two-word name "Black Hawks" was officially changed to the single word "Blackhawks.")

While the name was a nod to McLaughlin's personal history, the team's iconic logo bore a more intricate and communal narrative. From the onset, the side profile of a Native American, inspired by the Sauk war leader Black Hawk, became a defining image for the franchise. Its detailed crafting represented a nod to the rich tapestry of native histories in Illinois.

The team's inaugural season in the NHL was 1926-1927. For a brand-new franchise, the Blackhawks showed promise by making the playoffs. However, as with many new teams, they faced their share of growing pains. It was a time of adjustment, learning, and understanding the nuances of the league.

The early years were marked by frequent changes in the roster and coaching staff. Yet, the building blocks for future greatness were steadily being laid down. The Blackhawks played their home games at the Chicago Coliseum before moving to the larger Chicago Stadium in 1929, which would be their home for the next six decades. Known for its intimidating atmosphere, the Chicago Stadium became a fortress for the team, a place where magic was conjured on ice.

Key players emerged during these foundational years, with names like Johnny Gottselig, Mush March, and Charlie Gardiner becoming etched into Blackhawks lore. Gardiner, in particular, was a beacon of hope for the team. Hailing from Scotland and playing as a goaltender, his skills between the pipes were unparalleled. Under his leadership, the Blackhawks clinched their first Stanley Cup in 1934, a mere eight years after their formation.

The victory wasn't just about hoisting a trophy; it was emblematic of Chicago's resilience, dedication, and unyielding spirit. A team that started as newcomers in a league filled with established giants had carved their name on hockey's most coveted prize.

In reflection, the origins and foundational years of the Chicago Blackhawks were not just about statistics, wins, or losses. They were about a city discovering its love for a sport, a team finding its identity, and players who, with every pass, check, and goal, wove themselves into the heart of Chicago. Today, as fans don the jersey adorned with the iconic logo, they don't just support a team; they celebrate a legacy birthed in those early years of passion and perseverance.

Stadium Histories: From the Hallowed Halls of Chicago Stadium to the Modern Majesty of the United Center

Nestled in the heart of the Windy City, Chicago Stadium once stood as a colossus, resonating with the roars of fans and echoing with the memories of countless iconic moments. Today, while the Chicago Stadium is no longer standing, its legacy lives on through its successor, the United Center, ensuring that the spirit of Chicago's sports enthusiasm remains unbroken.

Built in 1929, the Chicago Stadium was more than just bricks and mortar; it was the beating heart of Chicago sports. Located on West Madison Street, the stadium was affectionately dubbed the "Madhouse on Madison" due to the deafening noise levels that the passionate Blackhawks fans consistently generated. Its architecture, featuring a grandiose pipe organ – the largest of its kind in the world at the time – gave games an almost cinematic feel, adding gravitas to every puck drop, every goal, and every save.

The memories etched within the confines of Chicago Stadium are plentiful. From the first time the Blackhawks took to its ice in 1929, the arena bore witness to their 1934 and 1938 Stanley Cup victories. It wasn't just the championships, though; it was the countless games, the playoff battles, the overtime thrillers, and the moments of pure, unbridled sportsmanship that made the stadium iconic.

But as with all great things, time took its toll on the Chicago Stadium. By the late 1980s, while it remained a beloved institution, the need for a more modern facility became evident. As sports evolved and fans' expectations shifted, the vision for a new, state-of-the-art arena began to take shape.

Enter the United Center. Inaugurated in 1994 and situated a stone's throw away from its predecessor, the United Center represented a seamless blend of tradition and modernity. Financed jointly by the Blackhawks and the NBA's Chicago Bulls, the facility was a testament to Chicago's commitment to remaining at the forefront of the sports world. Boasting a larger seating capacity, luxury suites, and cutting-edge amenities, the United Center was not just a stadium; it was an experience.

The transition was bittersweet for many. While fans marveled at the advancements of the United Center, there was an undeniable nostalgia for the old "Madhouse." Recognizing this, the designers of the United Center made deliberate efforts to pay homage to the Chicago Stadium. One of the most touching tributes was the installation of the old stadium's mighty brass horn, ensuring that goals scored by the Blackhawks in their new home would be celebrated with the same triumphant blast familiar to generations of fans.

Since its inception, the United Center has seen the Blackhawks rise to incredible heights, witnessing three Stanley Cup victories in 2010, 2013, and 2015. It has continued the tradition of serving as hallowed ground for sports in Chicago, echoing the legacy of the Chicago Stadium.

In essence, the tale of Chicago Stadium and the United Center is not merely about two buildings; it's a narrative of continuity, of honoring the past while embracing the future. It's about a city's undying love for its teams and the sanctuaries they call home. The echoes of skates on ice, the cheers of fans, and the thrill of victory – these are the constants, whether in the historic halls of Chicago Stadium or the modern corridors of the United Center.

Stanley Cup Sagas: The Blackhawks' Triumphant Tales on Ice

The Chicago Blackhawks have a storied history, filled with grit, determination, and moments of sheer brilliance. While every game holds its own narrative, the chapters that truly define the Blackhawks are their Stanley Cup victories. Each championship represents not only a win for the team but an emblem of hope, pride, and jubilation for the entire city.

1934: The First Triumph The Blackhawks' journey to their first Stanley Cup was nothing short of remarkable. After a strong regular season, they found themselves battling fiercely in the playoffs. Goalie Charlie Gardiner's presence was instrumental. Despite facing personal health challenges, Gardiner's unmatched skill between the pipes anchored the team. When the Blackhawks met the Detroit Red Wings in the finals, it was a contest of wills. After a series of nail-biting games, the Blackhawks emerged victorious in the final match, winning 1-0 in double overtime. Tragically, Gardiner would pass away just weeks later, making this victory a poignant memory in the team's history.

1938: Against All Odds The 1938 win stands as one of the most unexpected and thrilling chapters in Stanley Cup history. The Blackhawks ended the regular season with a less than stellar record, but what they lacked in points, they made up for in heart. Rallying together, they managed to upset favored teams to reach the finals against the Toronto Maple Leafs. In a turn of events that could only be described as cinematic, the Blackhawks clinched the Cup in Game 4. The team's sheer tenacity and undying spirit marked this victory, proving that underdogs could have their day.

1961: Breaking the Drought After 23 long years without a Cup, the Blackhawks were hungry for victory in 1961. With legendary players like Bobby Hull, Stan Mikita, and Glenn Hall in their ranks, the team showcased a mix of youth, experience, and sheer talent. Facing the Detroit Red Wings in the finals, the Blackhawks dominated, taking the series in six games. This win was particularly sweet for fans who had waited over two decades to see their team lift the Cup once more.

2010, 2013, and 2015: The Modern Dynasty The turn of the 21st century ushered in a golden era for the Blackhawks. After years of struggles, the team, bolstered by stars like Jonathan Toews, Patrick Kane, and Duncan Keith, became a force to be reckoned with.

In 2010, after an exhilarating playoff run, the Blackhawks faced the Philadelphia Flyers in the finals. Game 6, with the Blackhawks leading the series 3-2, ended in dramatic fashion as Kane scored the Cup-winning goal in overtime.

2013's victory against the Boston Bruins was equally heart-stopping. Down 2-1 in the final moments of Game 6, the Blackhawks staged an incredible comeback, scoring two goals in 17 seconds to clinch the Cup.

Two years later, in 2015, the Blackhawks showcased their prowess once more, defeating the Tampa Bay Lightning in six games. This victory solidified their status as a modern dynasty, with three Cup wins in six years.

In essence, each Stanley Cup saga of the Chicago Blackhawks isn't just about hoisting a trophy; it's about the players who gave their all, the fans who never stopped believing, and the indomitable spirit of a team that, time and again, has proven its mettle on the ice.

Blackhawks Legends: Celebrating the Icons of Chicago's Ice

The Chicago Blackhawks' illustrious history is punctuated by moments of brilliance, many of which were crafted by legendary players who donned the team's iconic jersey. Among the pantheon of greats, three names resonate deeply: Bobby Hull, Stan Mikita, and Tony Esposito. Each brought a unique flair, skill set, and passion to the ice, forever etching their names into the annals of Blackhawks lore.

Bobby Hull: The Golden Jet Radiating charisma and possessing an unmatched prowess on the ice, Bobby Hull was nothing short of a phenomenon. Nicknamed "The Golden Jet" due to his blonde hair and blistering speed, Hull's impact was immediate and profound. His slapshot was the stuff of legends, often leaving goalies frozen in awe as the puck zoomed past them. Over his 15 seasons with the Blackhawks, Hull not only racked up impressive statistics but also revolutionized the game with his athleticism and flair. He was an integral part of the 1961 Stanley Cup-winning team and remains, to this day, one of the most celebrated figures in the sport.

Stan Mikita: The Gentleman Playmaker While Hull's brilliance was explosive, Stan Mikita's was cerebral and graceful. Mikita's game was defined by intelligence, precision, and an uncanny ability to read plays before they unfolded. His playmaking skills were unparalleled, and he had a knack for setting up teammates in perfect scoring positions. But what set Mikita apart was his transformation as a player. Initially known for his aggressive style, he remarkably shifted to become one of the cleanest players, winning the Lady Byng Trophy for sportsmanship multiple times. Off the ice, Mikita's contributions were just as significant. He co-founded the American Hearing Impaired Hockey Association with former NHLer Irv Tiahnybik, a testament to his character and commitment to giving back.

Tony Esposito: Tony O, the Goalie Maestro In the realm of goaltenders, few names shine as brightly as Tony Esposito. "Tony O," as fans affectionately called him, was a bastion of reliability for the Blackhawks. With his distinctive butterfly style, Esposito could stymie even the most potent offenses. His rookie season with the Blackhawks was nothing short of magical. Recording 15 shutouts, he set a modern-day record and instantly endeared himself to the Chicago faithful. Esposito's tenure with the Blackhawks spanned an impressive 15 seasons, during which he was consistently among the league's elite goaltenders. His number 35 jersey, now retired, is a testament to his lasting impact on the franchise.

Each of these legends brought more than just skill to the ice; they brought a passion, a commitment, and an identity. Bobby Hull's electrifying runs, Stan Mikita's graceful playmaking, and Tony Esposito's unwavering presence in goal are more than just memories; they are chapters in a legacy. A legacy that has been built shot by shot, save by save, game by game.

The Chicago Blackhawks' tapestry is rich and diverse, and while many hands have woven it, the indelible imprints of Hull, Mikita, and Esposito are unmistakable. They are not just legends; they are the very soul of a team and a city that cherishes its heroes.

Coaching Chronicles: Steering the Ship with Billy Reay and Joel Quenneville

The trajectory of a sports team, while shaped by the athletes on the field or ice, is often deeply influenced by the minds orchestrating their movements from behind the bench. For the Chicago Blackhawks, two names stand out as coaching titans: Billy Reay and Joel Quenneville. While both helmed the team in different eras, their leadership, styles, and impact have left indelible marks on the franchise's storied history.

Billy Reay: The Strategic Maestro Taking the reins in 1963, Billy Reay would become the longest-serving coach in Blackhawks history, a testament to his longevity and effectiveness. Coming into a team with recent success, having won the Stanley Cup in 1961, Reay was tasked with the challenge of maintaining that momentum. And he did so with aplomb.

Reay's style was characterized by an analytical approach, often dissecting the game into its finer elements and crafting strategies that exploited the opposition's weaknesses. He was a pioneer in many respects, being among the first to frequently use video analysis, constantly evolving and adapting his tactics.

Under his guidance, the Blackhawks would reach the Stanley Cup Finals three times in the 1970s. While the ultimate prize eluded him, Reay's teams were perennial contenders, always in the mix and feared by opponents. Beyond his tactical acumen, Reay was known for his ability to instill discipline and structure, creating teams that were organized and efficient on the ice.

Joel Quenneville: The Modern Day Legend Fast forward to the 21st century, and another coaching legend emerges in the form of Joel Quenneville. Taking charge in 2008, Quenneville, affectionately known as "Coach Q," would lead a Blackhawks resurgence that saw them clinch three Stanley Cups in six years.

Quenneville's style was a blend of old-school grit and modern sensibilities. He demanded hard work and commitment from his players but was also known for his player-first approach. Coach Q was a master at managing personalities, ensuring that stars like Jonathan Toews and Patrick Kane coexisted harmoniously with role players. His line juggling, a frequent tactic, often seemed like a maestro conducting an orchestra, making subtle adjustments that often changed the course of games.

Under Quenneville, the Blackhawks played an aggressive, up-tempo style of hockey. They were relentless on the puck, with a defense that transitioned swiftly into offense. His tenure was marked by a blend of tactical brilliance and an unwavering commitment to a winning culture.

Both Reay and Quenneville, while leading in different eras, showcased an ability to adapt. Reay's embrace of video analysis and Quenneville's knack for lineup adjustments were testament to their forward-thinking approaches. They also shared an innate ability to command respect, forging deep connections with their players, which translated to on-ice success.

In the annals of Blackhawks history, while players often grab the headlines, the shadow of these coaching giants looms large. Billy Reay and Joel Quenneville, with their distinct styles and philosophies, sculpted eras of Blackhawks hockey, ensuring that the roar of the Madhouse on Madison never dimmed. Their legacy is not just in wins or Cups but in the culture, ethos, and identity they instilled in one of hockey's most iconic franchises.

Rivalries Renewed: Blackhawks' Battles Against the Original Six and Beyond

The heartbeat of any sports team, apart from its own victories and losses, often resonates with the intensity of its rivalries. For the Chicago Blackhawks, their long-standing history in the NHL, especially as a member of the prestigious Original Six, has seen them forge fierce competitions that have thrilled fans for decades. From brutal physical contests to chess-like strategic duels, these rivalries have added layers of drama and passion to the sport.

1. Chicago vs. Detroit: The Red Wings Rumble Perhaps the most iconic rivalry in Blackhawks history is with the Detroit Red Wings. As two of the Original Six teams located close geographically, their competition is as much about city pride as it is about hockey supremacy. Over the years, the Blackhawks and Red Wings have met in countless regular-season battles and playoff showdowns, with each game a testament to the intensity and passion of both sets of players and fans. While the Red Wings' move to the Eastern Conference in 2013 reduced their regular meetings, the fire of this rivalry will never truly dim.

2. Chicago vs. Toronto: Maple Leafs Melee Another classic Original Six rivalry, the Blackhawks' contests against the Toronto Maple Leafs, have been marked by their sheer unpredictability. With both teams boasting periods of dominance throughout NHL history, their clashes often have wider implications for the standings. As two of the most storied franchises in the league, their matchups are always awaited with bated breath by fans of the sport.

3. Chicago vs. St. Louis: The Blues Battle While not part of the Original Six, the rivalry between the Blackhawks and the St. Louis Blues is as intense as any. Given their proximity and frequent meetings, especially in the Central Division, these games often carry an added weight. Over

the years, the two teams have had several playoff encounters, each more intense than the last, forging a rivalry that often borders on the brutal. The sound of the Blackhawks' goal horn, "Chelsea Dagger," has become a particular point of contention, either a source of joy or irritation depending on which side of the rivalry one stands.

4. Chicago vs. Boston: The Bruins Brawl The Boston Bruins, another Original Six member, have had their fair share of clashes with the Blackhawks. While not as frequent as some other rivalries, their encounters are always high-stakes affairs. The 2013 Stanley Cup Final, where the Blackhawks defeated the Bruins in a thrilling six-game series, added a modern chapter to this age-old competition.

5. Chicago vs. Montreal: Canadiens Confrontation Meetings with the Montreal Canadiens, the most successful team in NHL history in terms of Stanley Cups won, are always a litmus test for the Blackhawks. Their clashes offer a blend of skill, speed, and strategy, a showcase of hockey at its very best.

These rivalries, steeped in history and passion, are about more than just the games. They are about the narratives, the heroes and villains, the moments of magic and heartbreak. For the Blackhawks, each of these rivalries has helped shape their identity, offering challenges that have, over the years, brought out the best in the team.

In the end, while the pursuit of the Stanley Cup remains the ultimate goal, the journey is made all the more thrilling by these fierce competitions. Rivalries, with their drama and intensity, ensure that the heart of the Blackhawks—and their fans—beats strong, game after game, season after season.

The Roaring Crowd: The Heartbeat of the Blackhawks

The bright lights of the stadium, the echoing chants, the sea of red jerseys—these are the markers of a Blackhawks game day. But what truly sets the Chicago Blackhawks apart from other teams isn't just the prowess displayed on the ice, but the unyielding passion of its fan base that fills the stands. The roaring crowd of Blackhawks supporters is the lifeblood of the franchise, providing a home advantage that many teams envy.

The Madhouse on Madison The United Center, fondly known as the "Madhouse on Madison," is more than just a venue; it's an experience. Anyone who's been fortunate enough to attend a game will attest to the electrifying atmosphere that pulsates through the arena. From the spine-tingling rendition of the National Anthem, where the roaring crowd drowns out even the organ, to the rhythmic claps and chants that echo throughout the game, Blackhawks fans ensure their presence is felt—not just by their own team, but by the opposition.

More Than Just Fans Blackhawks fans are a unique blend of loyalty, knowledge, and passion. Many have followed the team through thick and thin, from the championship highs to the rebuilding lows. This unwavering support has often been a beacon for the team, a reminder that the city stands behind them no matter the scoreline.

But it's not just about loud cheers and team jerseys. The fans showcase an in-depth understanding of the game. They appreciate a well-timed pass, a crucial block, and even the strategic nuance of a line change. This knowledgeable base adds a layer of depth to their support, making their cheers—and jeers—all the more poignant.

The 17-Second Magic If one were to encapsulate the spirit of the Blackhawks fan base, it would be hard to find a better moment than Game 6 of the 2013 Stanley Cup Final. Trailing 2-1 with less than two minutes to go, the situation seemed dire. But then, in a span of 17 seconds, the Blackhawks scored twice, taking the lead and eventually the Cup. The roar of the Blackhawks fans, both in the arena and thousands of miles away in Chicago, was deafening. It was a testament to the belief, hope, and sheer passion that the fans bring every time the team takes to the ice.

A Legacy of Support The legacy of the Blackhawks isn't just built on the stickwork of its players or the strategies of its coaches. It's crafted in the stands, in the bars, in the homes of every fan who dons the jersey and believes in the team. The roaring crowd is a constant reminder of the rich history and tradition of the Blackhawks—a history written not just by the players but by every supporter who ever believed in the magic of the team.

Conclusion In the end, while goals are scored on the ice, games are often won in the stands. The significance and influence of the Blackhawks' passionate fan base cannot be overstated. They are the 7th player, the extra push, the wind beneath the team's wings. In the cacophony of cheers, in the sea of red and black, in the undying hope of every game, lies the true strength of the Chicago Blackhawks—the roaring crowd that never stops believing.

Draft Day Diamonds: Unearthing Blackhawks' Gems Through the Years

The NHL Draft: a day of hopes, dreams, and the potential promise of future superstars. For the Chicago Blackhawks, their draft history is a treasure trove of talent, filled with choices that have sculpted the franchise's destiny. These draft day diamonds have not just filled roster spots but have become cornerstones, their impact echoing through the annals of Blackhawks' history.

1. Denis Savard (1980, 1st round, 3rd overall) Denis Savard's selection in the 1980 draft marked the dawn of a new era for the Blackhawks. Known for his Savardian Spin-o-Rama move, his skill, speed, and creativity brought a unique flair to the team. During his tenure, Savard would become one of the most beloved players in Blackhawks history, racking up impressive point totals and leaving fans in awe of his on-ice magic.

2. Steve Larmer (1980, 6th round, 120th overall) In the same draft as Savard, but in the shadows of the earlier rounds, Steve Larmer emerged as one of the most significant steals for the Blackhawks. His consistency and work ethic became the stuff of legends. Larmer's consecutive games streak, coupled with his scoring prowess, made him a foundational piece for the Blackhawks through the 1980s and early '90s.

3. Jeremy Roenick (1988, 1st round, 8th overall) When the Blackhawks drafted Jeremy Roenick, they acquired a player with not only skill but unparalleled charisma. Roenick's flair for the dramatic—both on and off the ice—endeared him to fans. His mix of scoring touch and physical play added depth and versatility to the Blackhawks' offensive arsenal.

4. Duncan Keith (2002, 2nd round, 54th overall) Arguably one of the best defensemen of his generation, Duncan Keith's selection in the second round of the 2002 draft was a masterstroke. With his impeccable

skating and innate ability to read the game, Keith became the defensive anchor for the Blackhawks. His crucial goals and tireless minutes, especially during the team's three Stanley Cup wins in the 2010s, underscore his draft day value.

5. Jonathan Toews (2006, 1st round, 3rd overall) & Patrick Kane (2007, 1st round, 1st overall) These back-to-back first-round picks transformed the Blackhawks' fortunes. Toews, with his leadership, two-way play, and clutch performances, and Kane, with his dazzling skills and game-winning heroics, became the faces of the franchise. Their impact has been monumental, leading the team to multiple Stanley Cups and ensuring the Blackhawks' place among the league's elite.

6. Brandon Saad (2011, 2nd round, 43rd overall) While not as heralded as some other picks, Saad's importance can't be understated. His versatility, be it his scoring touch or his ability to play in multiple roles, provided the Blackhawks with valuable depth during their championship runs.

The NHL Draft is often seen as a gamble, a mix of scouting, luck, and foresight. But for the Blackhawks, it's been a consistent source of talent and hope. From the early round certainties to the hidden gems unearthed in the later rounds, Chicago's draft day decisions have shaped the team's present and future.

In the grand tapestry of the Blackhawks' storied history, these draft day diamonds shine brightly, each pick a chapter in the ongoing saga of success, challenges, and undying passion for the game.

Mascot and Logo Evolution: The Journey of the Chicago Blackhawks' Branding and Representation

In the vast realm of sports, a team's logo and mascot are more than just symbolic representations. They carry with them the essence of the team's spirit, ethos, and history. For the Chicago Blackhawks, one of the NHL's Original Six teams, their branding journey is filled with rich history and meaningful evolution. Delving into this progression offers insights into both the team's heritage and the broader societal changes over time.

Origins: The Black Hawk Legacy The Blackhawks' name was inspired by the Black Hawk Division of the U.S. Army, a unit with which the team's original owner, Frederic McLaughlin, served during World War I. This division was named in honor of Chief Black Hawk, a leader of the Sauk Native American tribe. The early iterations of the logo, introduced in the 1920s, featured a detailed side profile of a Native American figure, reflecting this historical connection.

Logo Evolution: Adapting to the Times Over the decades, the Blackhawks' logo has seen several refinements, each capturing the essence of its time:

1930s-50s: The profile of the Native American figure was gradually simplified and stylized. These versions of the logo emphasized a more streamlined and iconic appearance.

1950s-Present: The logo transitioned from a side profile to the more familiar front-facing headshot of the Native American, with vibrant colors of red, black, green, yellow, and white. This design, while tweaked slightly over the years, has largely remained consistent and is one of the most recognizable logos in the NHL today.

Mascot Introduction: Enter Tommy Hawk In 2001, the Blackhawks introduced their official mascot, Tommy Hawk, a playful anthropomorphic black hawk who has since become a beloved figure at games and events. His energetic antics and crowd interactions offer a spirited and family-friendly dimension to the Blackhawks' brand, serving as an ambassador for the team off the ice.

Controversies and Cultural Sensitivities While the Blackhawks' logo is celebrated by many fans for its iconic design, it hasn't been without its share of controversy. As societal awareness about cultural representation grew, some critics pointed out that the logo might perpetuate Native American stereotypes. The Blackhawks, in response, have stated that they continue to strive for the logo to honor and teach about Native American history and heritage.

Over the years, the organization has been engaged in outreach and collaborations with Native American communities, aiming for a respectful representation and fostering mutual understanding. The team's dedication to ensuring that their branding respects the legacy of Chief Black Hawk and the broader Native American community is indicative of an evolving consciousness about the responsibilities that come with such representation.

The evolution of the Chicago Blackhawks' mascot and logo isn't just a tale of design changes; it's a reflection of the team's journey through different eras. From its military-inspired origins to its current status as an iconic sports brand, every iteration tells a story. Balancing respect for heritage with contemporary cultural sensibilities, the Blackhawks' branding stands as a testament to the team's enduring legacy and its commitment to moving forward with awareness and honor. In the fluid dance of history, tradition, and representation, the Chicago Blackhawks continue to carve out a path that respects both their storied past and the promise of the future.

Game-Changing Moments: A Walk Through the Unforgettable Milestones in Chicago Blackhawks' History

The Chicago Blackhawks' legacy is not just etched in their Stanley Cup victories or the legends who wore the jersey. It's equally embedded in those fleeting moments—iconic plays, turning points, and unforgettable games that shifted the trajectory of the team and left an indelible mark on the hearts of their fans. Let's journey through some of these game-changing moments that have defined the Blackhawks' storied history.

1. The 1961 Stanley Cup Victory

For a team that hadn't tasted Stanley Cup success since 1938, the 1961 victory was a monumental lift. The Blackhawks' defeat of the Detroit Red Wings in six games was punctuated by Reggie Fleming's iconic goal in Game 6. That victory broke a 23-year championship drought and showcased a young, dynamic team ready to make its mark.

2. Bobby Hull's 51st Goal (1966)

Bobby Hull, the "Golden Jet," was already an icon, but on March 12, 1966, he further cemented his legend status. With a slapshot that scorched past the New York Rangers' goalie, Hull became the first NHL player to score more than 50 goals in a season, finishing the campaign with 54.

3. The Savardian Spin-o-Rama

Denis Savard's Spin-o-Rama move is not just a moment but an era. This signature move, where Savard would spin completely around to evade a defender, left fans and opponents dazzled. While it's hard to pinpoint a single instance, his Spin-o-Rama against the Edmonton Oilers in the 1988 playoffs is etched in the memories of many.

4. 17 Seconds in 2013

Perhaps the most dramatic ending to a Stanley Cup Final in recent memory. Trailing 2-1 in Game 6 against the Boston Bruins with under two minutes left, Bryan Bickell tied the game. Merely 17 seconds later, Dave Bolland scored, giving the Blackhawks a lead they wouldn't relinquish. Those 17 seconds epitomized the never-say-die spirit of the 2013 team and secured their fifth Stanley Cup.

5. Patrick Kane's Phantom Goal (2010)

In overtime of Game 6 against the Philadelphia Flyers in the 2010 Stanley Cup Final, Patrick Kane shot the puck from a sharp angle. The puck disappeared, and for a moment, time stood still. Kane knew he'd scored, but it took a few seconds for the reality to dawn on everyone else. That goal sealed the Blackhawks' first championship in 49 years.

6. "The Shift" by Duncan Keith (2010)

During the 2010 Western Conference Finals against the San Jose Sharks, Duncan Keith showcased why he's among the elite defensemen in NHL history. After losing seven teeth from a puck to the face, Keith didn't just return to the game; he played a mammoth shift, blocking shots and making key plays, epitomizing the resilience of the Blackhawks.

7. Roenick's Tearful Tribute (1994)

After an agonizing Game 7 loss to the Vancouver Canucks in the 1994 playoffs, Jeremy Roenick, playing through injuries, gave a tearful post-game interview. His raw emotion showcased the deep bond between the players and the city, making it a poignant moment in Blackhawks' lore.

8. Seabrook's OT Winner (2013)

In the 2013 playoffs' first round, the Blackhawks faced potential elimination against the Detroit Red Wings. Down 3-1 in the series, the Blackhawks rallied back to force a Game 7. In overtime, defenseman Brent Seabrook surged forward, firing a shot that found the net, completing the comeback and paving the way for their eventual Stanley Cup win.

9. Hossa's 500th Goal (2016)

Marian Hossa, a linchpin for the Blackhawks during their three recent Cup wins, scored his 500th career goal in October 2016. His individual brilliance, combined with his team spirit, made this milestone a significant marker in the Blackhawks' recent dominance.

10. Tony Esposito's 15 Shutouts (1969-1970)

Rookie goaltender Tony Esposito stunned the NHL in the 1969-1970 season by recording a staggering 15 shutouts, setting a modern-day record. His brick-wall performances throughout that season are legendary moments that showcased the emergence of a goaltending icon.

While these game-changing moments offer snapshots of the Blackhawks' rich history, their true significance lies in the emotions they evoke. They remind fans of where they were, who they were with, and how they felt when history was being written. The blend of joy, heartbreak, hope, and exhilaration that these moments provide is a testament to the deep-rooted love and passion for the Chicago Blackhawks. In the end, it's not just about the goals scored or games won; it's about the journey, the memories, and the eternal bond between a team and its fans.

Behind-the-Scenes with the Chicago Blackhawks: A Glimpse into the Heartbeat of a Hockey Dynasty

Many see the glitz and glamour of game day—the dazzling plays, the roaring crowd, and the tension of a last-minute goal. But behind the spectacle lie hours of meticulous planning, grueling training, and intense camaraderie. Here's an exclusive behind-the-scenes look at the day-to-day operations of the Chicago Blackhawks, a journey that traverses the locker room, the gym, and the strategic huddles.

Morning Routines: The Day Begins The sun may still be yawning, but the United Center, or whatever away arena they might be in, is abuzz by 7:00 AM. Players start trickling in, grabbing light breakfasts catered by the team's nutritionists. Eggs, oatmeal, fruits, and the essential morning coffee fill the tables. Nutrition plays a crucial role, with each meal tailored to the specific needs and preferences of players.

Training Sessions: Where Games are Won After breakfast, it's time to hit the ice. Morning skates, often open to media, are less about intensity and more about tactics. Coaches run specific drills, focusing on areas of improvement identified from previous games. The atmosphere is a blend of concentration and camaraderie—teammates encouraging each other, interspersed with friendly banter.

Goalies often work separately with their specialized coaches, honing reflexes and shot-stopping techniques. Off the ice, there are weight training and physiotherapy sessions. The Blackhawks' training regimen is a precise science, balancing endurance, strength, and skill training.

Team Meetings: The Tactical Arena Post-training, players congregate for team meetings. This is where strategy takes center stage. Using a mix of data analytics and video footage, coaches break down the strengths and weaknesses of their next opponent, planning tactics down to the minutest detail. Players are engaged, asking questions, suggesting plays, and ensuring they're aligned on the game plan.

Lunch and Downtime: Refueling and Relaxation Lunchtime is both about refueling and relaxation. Players grab hearty meals—carbohydrates for energy, proteins for muscle recovery, and greens for overall health. Post-lunch, players get some downtime. Some prefer a short nap, some engage in light reading or gaming, while others might indulge in friendly card games or jokes, building that essential locker room camaraderie.

The Locker Room: The Sanctum of Brotherhood The locker room is more than just a place to change. It's the sanctum of team spirit. Pictures from historic wins, motivational quotes, and mementos from landmark games adorn the walls. Each player's stall is personalized, often with tokens from their personal life—a child's drawing, a note from a loved one.

As game time nears, the locker room dynamics shift from relaxed to intensely focused. There's a palpable tension, a blend of nerves and excitement. Veteran players often share words of encouragement, reminding everyone of the jersey's weight and history.

Game Time: The Culmination All the day's preparations culminate in those intense 60 minutes on the ice. Players, now in full gear, line up to storm the rink. There's a final huddle, a rallying cry, and then the spectacle unfolds.

Post-Game: Reflection and Recovery Post-game, win or lose, is a time for reflection. Players cool down, tend to injuries, and engage in recovery therapies. There are media obligations, interviews, and press conferences. Coaches and players review the game, identifying areas of improvement.

But more than anything, it's a time for the team to come together, appreciating each other's efforts.

The day in the life of a Chicago Blackhawks player is more than just about hockey. It's a carefully orchestrated blend of preparation, strategy, brotherhood, and reflection. The roaring crowd sees the final product, the on-ice spectacle, but behind it lies a world driven by passion, dedication, and an unwavering commitment to excellence. The behind-the-scenes world of the Blackhawks offers a poignant reminder: it's not just the goals, saves, or tackles that define a game; it's the heartbeat, the soul, and the spirit behind every move.

The Captaincy: Leading the Chicago Blackhawks, On and Off the Ice

In the dynamic and fast-paced world of hockey, leadership is paramount. It's not merely about scoring goals or making saves; it's about steering the team, setting the tone, and leading by example. For the Chicago Blackhawks, a team steeped in history and tradition, the role of the captain is sacrosanct. Let's journey through the captaincy of the Blackhawks, exploring the men who wore the 'C' on their jerseys and how they've shaped the team's destiny both on and off the ice.

A Historical Perspective The Blackhawks' roster of captains reads like a roll call of hockey's greats. From the early years with Johnny Gottselig, who was the first captain to hoist a Stanley Cup for Chicago in 1934, to modern legends, the captaincy has been a blend of talent, character, and resilience.

Stan Mikita: The Gentleman Captain Wearing the captain's 'C' from 1961 to 1976, Stan Mikita exemplified what it meant to be a Blackhawk. He wasn't the loudest or the most boisterous, but his influence was undeniable. On the ice, he was prolific, becoming the franchise's all-time leading scorer. Off the ice, he was equally impactful, championing the cause for protective helmets and showcasing sportsmanship, even winning the Lady Byng Trophy twice.

Dirk Graham: Breaking Barriers In 1989, Dirk Graham made history by becoming the NHL's first captain of African descent. But his captaincy was more than just symbolic. Graham led with grit and determination, guiding the Blackhawks to a Stanley Cup Final in 1992. His leadership was about breaking barriers and setting new standards.

Jonathan Toews: Captain Serious Arguably one of the most recognizable faces in modern Blackhawks' history, Jonathan Toews, affectionately dubbed "Captain Serious," has been a bedrock of stability. Since being named captain in 2008, Toews has steered the Blackhawks to three Stanley Cup victories. His on-ice brilliance is matched only by his off-ice dedication. A vocal advocate for mental health and community involvement, Toews' leadership extends beyond the rink.

The Role of the Captain Wearing the 'C' isn't just about talent; it's a testament to the player's character, work ethic, and ability to rally the troops. The captain is the bridge between the coaching staff and the players, often acting as the voice of the locker room. In times of adversity, be it a losing streak or off-field challenges, the captain is the beacon, guiding and steadying the ship.

In the Blackhawks' ethos, the captaincy isn't just ceremonial. It demands accountability. Captains are expected to lead team meetings, mentor young players, and often, face the media, answering for the team's performance.

Off the Ice: Leading in the Community Beyond the goals, assists, and on-ice strategies, Blackhawks' captains have a legacy of community engagement. They're not just athletes; they're ambassadors, representing the team in charitable endeavors, community events, and youth programs. The captaincy is as much about community leadership as it is about hockey prowess.

The Weight of the 'C' To understand the gravity of the Blackhawks' captaincy, one needs to look no further than the raucous United Center. When the captain skates out, there's a palpable shift in energy, a mix of reverence and expectation. The 'C' is not just a letter on the jersey; it's a symbol of trust, responsibility, and the weight of history.

The Chicago Blackhawks' captaincy is a tapestry of talent, leadership, and legacy. It's about guiding the team through thick and thin, being the embodiment of its values, and carrying forward a storied tradition. From the early legends to the modern icons, Blackhawks' captains have been the cornerstone of the franchise, shaping its destiny with their leadership on and off the ice. In the end, the 'C' is more than just a designation; it's a commitment to excellence, a promise to the fans, and an ode to the legends who've come before.

Postseason Perseverance: The Grit and Glory of the Chicago Blackhawks' Playoff Journeys

In the universe of sports, few moments shimmer with as much allure as the NHL playoffs. It's a crucible of tension, talent, and tenacity. And for the Chicago Blackhawks, a team with a storied past, the playoffs are a tapestry of unforgettable moments, punctuated with exhilarating highs and agonizing lows. While the ultimate prize, the Stanley Cup, has been claimed by the Blackhawks multiple times, there's a deeper narrative—one of resilience, determination, and an unyielding spirit. Let's embark on a journey, highlighting the Blackhawks' most memorable playoff runs, including those where the Cup remained elusive.

1962 Stanley Cup Finals While the 1960s witnessed the Blackhawks clinch the Cup in 1961, the subsequent year's playoff run was just as memorable. The 1962 postseason saw Chicago reaching the finals, riding high on the brilliance of stars like Bobby Hull and Stan Mikita. In a fierce battle against the Toronto Maple Leafs, the Blackhawks showed resilience. Although they fell short in the finals, the heart and passion they displayed set the tone for the decade, cementing their reputation as perennial contenders.

1971 Stanley Cup Finals Flash forward to 1971, and the Blackhawks were once again in the spotlight, facing off against the Montreal Canadiens. With a young Tony Esposito guarding the net and a roster filled with talent, Chicago quickly surged to a 2-0 series lead. However, the Canadiens, led by rookie goaltender Ken Dryden, mounted a stunning comeback. The Blackhawks fought valiantly but eventually succumbed. Yet, this series was a testament to the team's fighting spirit, as they pushed a legendary Canadiens team to the brink.

1992: An Unexpected Surge The early 1990s were transformative for the Blackhawks. With coach Mike Keenan at the helm and players like Chris Chelios and Jeremy Roenick showcasing their prowess, the 1992 playoff run was nothing short of magical. The Blackhawks bulldozed through the early rounds, reaching the Stanley Cup Finals after a 49-year hiatus. While the Pittsburgh Penguins, led by Mario Lemieux, proved to be an insurmountable obstacle, Chicago's journey to the finals rekindled hope and pride in the Windy City.

2009: A Sign of Things to Come While the subsequent years saw the Blackhawks miss out on the ultimate prize, the 2009 playoff run was an indelible mark of the team's resurgence. With a young core featuring Jonathan Toews, Patrick Kane, and Duncan Keith, Chicago soared to the Western Conference Finals, eventually losing to the seasoned Detroit Red Wings. But this playoff run was more than just a series of games—it was a statement of intent, a precursor to the dynasty that was on the horizon.

2014 Western Conference Finals In the annals of modern hockey, few series are as riveting as the 2014 Western Conference Finals between the Blackhawks and the Los Angeles Kings. Reigning champions Chicago, with two Cups in the last four years, locked horns with a determined Kings side. The seven-game saga had everything: late-game heroics, overtime thrillers, and unparalleled drama. While the Kings edged out the Blackhawks in overtime of Game 7, the series solidified its place as one of the most exhilarating in NHL history. Chicago might have lost the battle, but their character and resilience won the hearts of many.

The Essence of Postseason Perseverance Each of these playoff runs, though not culminating in lifting the Stanley Cup, encapsulates what it means to be a Blackhawk. It's about pushing boundaries, overcoming adversity, and showcasing unyielding perseverance. It's the grit displayed by players, skating through injuries, blocking shots, and giving their all for the emblem on their jersey. It's the fans, filling the United Center (or the old Chicago Stadium), creating an electrifying atmosphere that sends shivers down the spine.

Postseason runs, irrespective of the outcome, are chapters in the rich narrative of a team's history. And for the Blackhawks, these runs are symbolic of their undying spirit. They showcase moments of sheer brilliance, instances of heartbreak, but above all, an unwavering determination to persevere.

The Chicago Blackhawks' legacy isn't just defined by the championships won but also by the battles fought. It's about the journey, the roller-coaster of emotions, and the indomitable will to forge ahead, regardless of the odds. While the glimmer of the Stanley Cup is undoubtedly enticing, the essence of hockey—and sports in general—lies in the pursuit. And as the Blackhawks' postseason sagas have shown, it's a pursuit characterized by passion, perseverance, and an undying love for the game.

So, here's to the Chicago Blackhawks—for not just the victories but for the relentless spirit, for the memorable playoff runs, and for epitomizing the essence of postseason perseverance. In the world of hockey, it's not just about the destination; it's about the journey. And what a journey it has been for the men in the red and black.

Changing of the Guard: The Evolution of Eras, Players, and Styles in Chicago Blackhawks History

The ever-evolving world of professional sports demands adaptation, innovation, and often a departure from the familiar. In the case of the Chicago Blackhawks, a franchise with deep roots in the annals of NHL history, these shifts are more than just strategic changes; they mark the changing of the guard, a transition between eras, players, and styles of play.

The Origins: The Traditionalists The Blackhawks' formation in 1926 was a nod to the traditional style of play — straightforward, physical, and defense-oriented. The game was slower, punctuated by bouts of intense physicality. During this era, the team's legends like Doc Romnes and Johnny Gottselig epitomized the spirit of old-school hockey.

The 60s & 70s: Rise of the Superstars As the decades rolled on, the Blackhawks underwent a profound transformation. The 60s and 70s ushered in an era of superstar players, with the likes of Bobby Hull, Stan Mikita, and Tony Esposito showcasing a blend of skill, finesse, and power. The team's style of play evolved, focusing more on offense, with breathtaking plays and impressive goal tallies. The NHL was also growing, with new teams and talent emerging, making adaptability a necessity.

80s & 90s: A Defensive Resurgence The late 80s and 90s saw the NHL shift towards a more defensively inclined game, with a significant emphasis on goaltending and defensive structures. Chicago wasn't left behind. With players like Chris Chelios patrolling the blue line and Ed Belfour guarding the net, the Blackhawks adapted, adopting a more systematic and structured approach to the game. Though offensive stalwarts like Jeremy Roenick ensured that the team's attacking verve was intact, the emphasis was clear: a solid defense.

2000s & 2010s: Speed and Skill Take Center Stage The new millennium marked yet another evolution in the NHL. The game became faster, driven by skillful playmaking and agility rather than brute strength. The Blackhawks, not to be left behind, saw a changing of the guard with young guns like Jonathan Toews, Patrick Kane, and Duncan Keith. These players brought with them a style of play characterized by speed, creativity, and finesse. This era also witnessed Chicago's resurgence as a dominant force, culminating in multiple Stanley Cup victories.

Changing Personnel: Beyond Just Players It wasn't just the players on the ice that signified a changing of the guard. Behind the bench, the leadership style of coaches like Billy Reay, Mike Keenan, and Joel Quenneville showcased adaptability in strategies, training regimens, and game-day tactics. Each coach brought with him a unique approach, be it Reay's old-school methods, Keenan's disciplinarian style, or Quenneville's balanced approach, blending youth with experience.

The Fans: Adapting to the Times A critical yet often overlooked component in the Blackhawks' transitions over the years is the fanbase. The raucous crowds at the Chicago Stadium and later at the United Center have been the team's twelfth man. As the style of play evolved, so did the fans' understanding and appreciation of the game. They cheered, jeered, and lived through every goal, save, and penalty, adapting to the changing tides of the game and embracing new heroes who donned the Blackhawks jersey.

The Importance of Evolution In a sport as dynamic as hockey, stagnation is a precursor to downfall. The Blackhawks' success over the years can be attributed to their ability to change, be it in playing style, personnel, or strategy. But these changes were never abrupt; they were seamless transitions, ensuring that while the team adapted to the demands of modern hockey, they never lost sight of their rich history and traditions.

The Chicago Blackhawks' journey, punctuated by different eras, players, and styles, is a testament to the franchise's resilience and adaptability. As the game of hockey evolved, so did the team, ensuring that they remained at the pinnacle of the sport. The changing of the guard, whether it's players passing the torch to the next generation or a shift in the style of play, is emblematic of the Blackhawks' enduring spirit.

Through all the changes, one thing remains constant: the undying passion for the game and the commitment to excellence. Whether it's the legends of yesteryears or the modern-day heroes, the essence of being a Blackhawk remains unchanged. It's about pride, passion, and an unwavering dedication to the crest. In the ever-changing landscape of the NHL, the Chicago Blackhawks stand tall, a beacon of adaptability, perseverance, and timeless excellence.

Off-Ice Impact: The Blackhawks' Benevolent Reach in Chicago's Communities

The essence of a sports team, especially one as storied as the Chicago Blackhawks, goes far beyond the confines of the rink. Its true value can often be gauged by the impact it makes off the ice, particularly in the communities it calls home. For the Blackhawks, their legacy in Chicago isn't limited to their on-ice triumphs; it extends into the very fabric of the city's neighborhoods, shining through their countless charitable endeavors and community outreach programs.

The Heartbeat of Chicago From the hustle of Downtown to the serene neighborhoods on the outskirts, Chicago is a city with a heartbeat echoing the rhythms of its diverse communities. Amidst this vibrant tapestry, the Blackhawks have carved a niche not just as a sports team, but as a community pillar. Their commitment to the Windy City's residents is evident in the multitude of community initiatives they've spearheaded over the decades.

The Chicago Blackhawks Foundation Central to the Blackhawks' off-ice endeavors is the Chicago Blackhawks Foundation. Established to serve the local community, the foundation has been instrumental in providing support to health, education, housing, and youth-access programs throughout Chicago. With millions of dollars in grants distributed annually, the Foundation is a testament to the Blackhawks' commitment to fostering positive change and growth in the community.

Educational Initiatives Understanding the importance of education in shaping the future, the Blackhawks have consistently prioritized educational initiatives. Programs like the "Reading: The Ultimate Power Play" encourages students to develop reading habits, while partnerships with organizations like "EVERFI" aim to foster essential life skills in students. These initiatives ensure that the youth of Chicago are given ample opportunities to succeed academically.

Health and Wellness Outreach Recognizing the importance of holistic wellness, the Blackhawks have also invested significantly in health programs. The "G.O.A.L. (Get Out And Learn)" initiative, for instance, introduces children to the basics of hockey, promoting physical fitness. Meanwhile, the team's support for organizations like the "Ann & Robert H. Lurie Children's Hospital" underscores their commitment to ensuring healthcare accessibility for all, especially the younger generation.

Youth Hockey Development The Blackhawks' passion for the sport doesn't stop at the professional level. They're deeply invested in sowing the seeds of hockey at the grassroots. Through clinics, training camps, and partnerships with local organizations, they've championed youth hockey in Chicago, ensuring that every child, irrespective of their background, gets an opportunity to experience the joy of the game.

Community Engagement Engaging directly with the community, the Blackhawks have also organized countless events, from neighborhood festivals to charity runs. The "Blackhawks Street Team" is often spotted around the city, interacting with fans, organizing games, and spreading the love of hockey. Furthermore, the annual "Blackhawks Convention" offers fans an opportunity to meet players, partake in panel discussions, and immerse themselves in all things Blackhawks, reinforcing the bond between the team and the city.

Supporting Veterans and First Responders The Blackhawks' community engagement also extends to honoring those who've served and continue to serve the nation and city. Through initiatives like "Hockey Fights Cancer" and special game nights dedicated to veterans and first responders, the Blackhawks pay homage to these heroes, acknowledging their sacrifices and contributions.

Environmental Initiatives In recent years, the Blackhawks have also championed environmental causes. Their "Go Green" game night is a testament to their commitment to sustainability, promoting eco-friendly practices and raising awareness about environmental issues.

The Ripple Effect The Blackhawks' commitment to Chicago is more than just monetary donations or isolated events; it's about creating a ripple effect of change. Their initiatives inspire other organizations and individuals to partake in charitable endeavors. The team's players often leverage their platform, embarking on personal charitable projects, amplifying the impact manifold.

The Chicago Blackhawks, in their illustrious history, have etched their name on the Stanley Cup multiple times, leaving an indelible mark on the NHL. But their legacy in Chicago isn't merely defined by their on-ice prowess. It's shaped by their unwavering commitment to the community, their relentless pursuit of positive change, and their deep-seated belief in giving back.

As the city of Chicago stands tall amidst its historic architecture, bustling streets, and serene lakeside, the spirit of the Blackhawks resonates in its alleys, schools, hospitals, and parks. Through their off-ice endeavors, the Blackhawks have proven that a sports team's true victory lies not just in the championships won but in the hearts touched, lives changed, and communities uplifted.

In the grand tapestry of Chicago's history, the Blackhawks emerge not just as a sports team but as a beacon of hope, resilience, and benevolence. Their off-ice impact is a testament to the adage that the true essence of a team lies not in its trophies but in its soul. And the soul of the

Blackhawks beats in harmony with the heart of Chicago, echoing tales of perseverance, passion, and profound impact.

Unique Traditions: The Heartbeat of Blackhawks' Legacy and the Echo of "Chelsea Dagger"

Sports, at their core, are more than just games. They're a tapestry of emotions, memories, and traditions that define the identity of a team and resonate with its fans. The Chicago Blackhawks, with their storied history, have cultivated a plethora of traditions that elevate the fan experience to a transcendental level. Among these, the unmistakable chords of "Chelsea Dagger" post a goal remain one of the most iconic and beloved. Let's dive deep into the origins and significance of this unique tradition and others that make the Blackhawks experience truly special.

The Allure of "Chelsea Dagger" The Fratellis' "Chelsea Dagger" has become synonymous with Blackhawks goals. Every time the puck finds the net for Chicago, the United Center reverberates with the song's catchy chorus. But how did this Scottish band's tune become the emblematic celebration anthem of one of the NHL's Original Six teams?

The story dates back to the late 2000s. The Blackhawks, in their bid to revamp fan experience, sought a distinctive song that could be played after each goal. After experimenting with several tracks, "Chelsea Dagger" was played during a preseason game in 2008. The infectious melody, combined with its upbeat tempo, instantly resonated with the fans, and the rest, as they say, is history.

But it's not just the catchy tune that made it a fan favorite. It represents a moment of collective triumph, a crescendo of emotions after the climax of a goal. The song has witnessed countless memorable goals, playoff victories, and three Stanley Cup wins, solidifying its place in Blackhawks folklore.

Beyond the Melody: The Significance of "Chelsea Dagger" Traditions in sports, particularly in hockey, transcend their superficial aspects. "Chelsea Dagger" isn't just a song; it's an embodiment of collective joy, camaraderie, and the unbreakable bond between the team and its fans. It's the audio cue that unites thousands in a synchronous celebration, a modern ritual that marks a moment of success. The joyous chorus is not only a taunt to the opposing team but a testament to the indomitable spirit of Blackhawks fans.

Other Cherished Blackhawks Traditions

While "Chelsea Dagger" stands out, the Blackhawks' heritage is rich with traditions that add layers to the team's identity.

1. The National Anthem Ovation: One of the most goosebump-inducing moments at the United Center is the rendition of the "Star-Spangled Banner" before the puck drop. Unlike the usual reverent silence observed during national anthems, Blackhawks fans are known for their roaring applause and cheers throughout the anthem, a tradition that dates back to the 1985 playoffs. It's a powerful moment, encapsulating pride, patriotism, and passion.

2. The Feathered Headdress: The Blackhawks' logo, featuring a Native American in a feathered headdress, is a nod to the team's namesake, Black Hawk, a leader of the Sauk nation. While the logo has been a point of contention and discussions about its appropriateness, it represents, for many fans, a symbol of respect, strength, and resilience.

3. The Annual Training Camp Festival: Every year, fans get a sneak peek into the team's preparations for the upcoming season during the Training Camp Festival. It's a day-long celebration where fans can watch open practices, partake in various activities, and bond over their shared love for the Blackhawks.

4. Player Rituals: Players, over the years, have had their quirks and pre-game rituals. From Patrick Kane's left skate-first tradition to Duncan Keith's specific warm-up routines, these idiosyncrasies add a personal touch, showcasing the players' superstitions, beliefs, and character.

In Conclusion: The Soul of the Blackhawks

Traditions in sports are more than mere rituals; they're the threads that weave the fabric of a team's legacy. For the Blackhawks, traditions like "Chelsea Dagger" and the national anthem ovation aren't just events during a game; they're experiences that leave an indelible mark on fans' hearts.

In the grand scheme of things, while trophies, records, and accolades are critical, it's these unique traditions that define the soul of a team. They capture the essence of fandom, encapsulating moments of joy, sorrow, hope, and despair.

"Chelsea Dagger" is not just a post-goal song; it's an anthem of victory, perseverance, and shared joy. Every time its chords echo in the United Center, it's a reminder of the countless memories etched in the annals of Blackhawks history. It's a tradition that binds generations of fans, a melody that transcends the game, and encapsulates the essence of being a Blackhawk.

As the years roll on and the team embarks on new journeys, these traditions will remain, evolving, yet constant, echoing the timeless legacy of the Chicago Blackhawks. They remind us that at the heart of every game, beyond strategies, scores, and statistics, it's the emotions, memories, and shared experiences that truly matter.

Connor Bedard: The Rising Star of the Hockey World

In the annals of hockey, every so often, a player emerges whose talent and potential captivate fans, players, and pundits alike. As of now, Connor Bedard stands as one of those exceptional talents, destined to leave an indelible mark on the world of ice hockey. A prodigy in every sense of the word, Bedard's journey from a young boy with a dream to one of the most sought-after talents in the sport is a testament to his skill, determination, and passion.

Born on July 17, 2005, in North Vancouver, British Columbia, Bedard's affinity for the sport became evident from a very young age. While most kids his age were still grappling with the basics of skating, young Connor was already showcasing a skill set that belied his years.

His journey into the competitive realm began with the West Vancouver Warriors of the Pacific Coast Bantam Hockey League (PCBHL). However, it was with the Regina Pats of the Western Hockey League (WHL) that Bedard truly began to turn heads. It is evident that joining the WHL was a pivotal turning point in his career.

In 2020, Bedard made history by becoming the first player ever to be granted exceptional player status for the WHL, allowing him to be drafted a year early at just 15 years of age. This distinction put him in an elite club of Canadian players, such as John Tavares, Aaron Ekblad, and Connor McDavid, who were bestowed with similar honors in the Ontario Hockey League.

During his rookie season with the Regina Pats, Bedard's prodigious talent was on full display. He dominated the ice, showcasing a blend of agility, vision, and an innate goal-scoring ability. Despite the challenges presented by the COVID-19 pandemic, Bedard's performance remained undeterred. He wrapped up the season with an impressive tally of 28 points in just 15 games, an achievement that earned him the WHL's Rookie of the Year award.

But it wasn't just within the WHL that Bedard's star shone brightly. He represented Canada at the U18 World Championships in 2021 and played a crucial role in guiding the team to gold. With 14 points in 7 games, he finished the tournament as Canada's top scorer and the third-highest overall. These numbers, at such a young age, on an international platform, underscore the magnitude of Bedard's talent.

His style of play, marked by a seamless blend of intelligence and skill, sets him apart from many of his contemporaries. Bedard possesses an uncanny ability to read the game, find spaces, and execute plays that many wouldn't even see. His puck-handling skills, combined with a sharp shooter's precision, make him a formidable force on the ice.

Off the ice, Bedard's maturity and humility further accentuate his uniqueness. Despite the media glare and the weight of expectations, he remains grounded, focused on his growth and the contributions he can make to his team. His teammates and coaches have often lauded not just his skills but also his work ethic, determination, and leadership qualities.

Given his trajectory, comparisons with hockey greats are inevitable. The echelons of the sport, where legends like Wayne Gretzky, Mario Lemieux, and Sidney Crosby reside, might soon witness the addition of Connor Bedard. While such comparisons and projections come with immense pressure, if there's anyone equipped to handle it and carve out his own unique legacy, it's Bedard.

Connor Bedard represents the future of Chicago Blackhawks hockey. A prodigious talent with a level-headed approach, he embodies the best of athleticism and sportsmanship. While the journey ahead is long and fraught with challenges, if his past performances are anything to go by, the hockey world is set for a treat. As fans, players, and enthusiasts, all we can do is sit back, enjoy, and bear witness to the rise of a legend in the making.

Legacy Beyond the Ice: The Timeless Spirit of the Chicago Blackhawks

As the sun sets over the Chicago skyline, casting a golden hue over the iconic edifices of the Windy City, the heartbeats of countless fans resonate with the age-old chants, songs, and memories of the Chicago Blackhawks. This journey, exploring the myriad facets of the team, from its origins to its traditions, has unveiled more than just historical events or iconic moments; it has unraveled the essence of what it means to be a part of the Blackhawks family.

The Chicago Blackhawks, beyond the glitz of their Stanley Cup victories and the legends that adorned their jerseys, are an institution. Their story is not confined to the cold expanse of the rink but spreads out, seeping into the very heart of Chicago. From the origins in 1926, with the birth of a team that would become a beacon for hockey in the Midwest, to the roaring crowds that define the electrifying atmosphere of their games, every chapter of their saga is a testament to passion, perseverance, and pride.

Their victories on the ice, while monumental, are but one dimension of their legacy. Off the ice, the Blackhawks have left an indelible mark, molding the character of a city that thrives on resilience and unity. Through their community initiatives, they've reached out, touched lives, and brought about change. The tales of their draft diamonds, the leadership sagas of their captains, and their charitable endeavors illuminate the team's commitment not just to the sport but to humanity.

Each game, each season is a symphony of emotions. The highs, the lows, the ecstasy of a game-winning goal, or the agony of a playoff defeat - these are moments that are etched in time, shared collectively by the team and its legion of fans. The unforgettable plays, the turning points, and the iconic moments like the echo of "Chelsea Dagger" are not just events but experiences, binding fans across generations.

However, the pulse of the Blackhawks is not merely in their memorable games or legendary players. It's found in the subtle nuances, the traditions that have evolved over the years. The electrifying rendition of the national anthem, the unique goal celebrations, and even the locker room dynamics offer a glimpse into the soul of the team. It's in these moments, these rituals, that one truly grasps the depth of the Blackhawks' legacy.

Every player, from the legends who have immortalized themselves in Blackhawks lore to the young draftees taking their first steps, carries forward a legacy. It's a legacy of not just playing hockey but of representing an ideal, an ethos rooted in dedication, teamwork, and community. The captaincy isn't merely a letter on a jersey; it's a mantle of leadership, a responsibility that transcends the game.

But perhaps the most poignant aspect of the Blackhawks' journey is its reflection in the eyes of its fans. From young children, eyes wide with wonder, watching their first game, to the elderly, who've witnessed the team's evolution over decades, the Blackhawks are more than just a team; they're an emotion, a part of one's very being.

As we conclude this exploration, it's evident that the Chicago Blackhawks are not just about moments of glory or defeat. They're about stories, stories of individuals, of a city, of fans. Stories of dreams, aspirations, heartbreaks, and jubilations. The history of the Blackhawks isn't just in the records or the statistics; it's in the collective memory of millions who've cheered, cried, celebrated, and despaired with the team.

In the grand tapestry of sports, the Chicago Blackhawks shine as a beacon, not just for their accomplishments but for their spirit. A spirit that captures the essence of Chicago, of hockey, and of humanity. As the chapters of their saga continue to unfold, one thing remains certain - the legacy of the Chicago Blackhawks, rich, profound, and timeless, will continue to inspire, uniting hearts and echoing the undying love for the game and the city they call home.

Don't miss out!

Visit the website below and you can sign up to receive emails whenever Lloyd Green publishes a new book. There's no charge and no obligation.

https://books2read.com/r/B-A-RYABB-JZBQC

BOOKS 2 READ

Connecting independent readers to independent writers.

Did you love *Original Six Era: The Rise of the Chicago Blackhawks Dynasty*? Then you should read *Chicago Bears Fun Facts*[1] by Trivia Ape!

[2]

Discover the ultimate fan experience with the "Chicago Bears Fun Facts" book – an exciting journey through the rich history and legendary moments of this iconic NFL team. Packed with over 1000 detailed fun facts, this family-friendly book is designed to challenge and entertain fans of all ages while deepening their knowledge of the Chicago Bears.

Immerse yourself in the heart-pounding action, unforgettable plays, and standout players that have defined their legacy. From thrilling rivalries and historic divisional matchups to legendary offensive star players and iconic stadium facts, each question provides a captivating glimpse into the team's remarkable journey.

---

1. https://books2read.com/u/3GGwz8

2. https://books2read.com/u/3GGwz8

Unearth captivating insights into the team origins, relive iconic victories, and celebrate the achievements of Hall of Fame players who have graced the field for this epic franchise. With a careful balance of challenging facts and accessible content, readers will learn fascinating facts, engage in spirited discussions, and proudly display their Chicago Bears expertise.

Whether you're a lifelong fan looking to increase your knowledge or a newcomer eager to learn about their storied past, the "Chicago Bears Fun Facts" book is your go-to source for immersive entertainment.

Read more at www.triviaape.com.

Also by Lloyd Green

Original Six Era: The Rise of the Chicago Blackhawks Dynasty